It's a Punderful Life

I'd say this book is
comparable to the work
of the great humorists
Molière and Wilde.

It's a Punderful Life

MAKE EVERY DAY A PUNDAY

Gemma Correll

I really dig these puns, man!

Yeah, groovy, baby.

DOG 'n' BONE

This edition published in 2023 by Dog 'n' Bone Books
An imprint of Ryland Peters & Small Ltd

20–21 Jockey's Fields   341 E 116th St
London WC1R 4BW   New York, NY 10029

www.rylandpeters.com

10 9 8 7 6 5 4 3 2 1

First published in 2014

Text © Gemma Correll 2014
Design © Dog 'n' Bone Books 2014

A CIP catalog record for this book is available from
the Library of Congress and the British Library.

ISBN: 978 1 912983 77 3

Printed in China

Editor: Pete Jorgensen
Designer: Jerry Goldie
Illustrator: Gemma Correll

Art director: Sally Powell
Creative director: Leslie Harrington
Head of production: Patricia Harrington
Publishing manager: Penny Craig
Publisher: Cindy Richards

THE PUNS

COMEDY GOLD

CRUSHED PINEAPPLE

A CORDIAL INVITATION

EMOTIONAL BAGGAGE

GANGSTER WRAP

DISTRESSED LEATHER

COMPLIMENTARY COLORS

MOOD SWINGS

LE PAIN

OUCH!

S&M&M

CURED MEATS

VICIOUS CYCLE

WONTON CRUELTY

HOW DO I KNOW
THAT MY EXPERIENCE OF
CONSCIOUSNESS IS THE SAME
AS ANOTHER'S EXPERIENCE
OF CONSCIOUSNESS?

WHY ARE
WE HERE?

WHAT IS MY
PURPOSE?

WHAT IS THE
MEANING OF LIFE?

COMPLEX
CARBOHYDRATES

BITTER COFFEE

GLAM ROCK

PETRIFIED FOREST

UNRELIABLE SAUCES

SHELF AWARENESS

BLUNT PENCIL

PEAR PRESSURE

SUPPORT BRAS

BORED GAMES

SIGH.

CATAGORIZING CATS

CAT À MERINGUE

CAT À LIST

CAT À TONIC

CAT À LOG

SOPHISTICATED PALETTE

WHAT'S THE PLATTER?

TRAY BIEN.

PAS TRAY BIEN.

CEREAL MONOGAMY

A PORPOISE IN LIFE

PORPOISE

MULTI PORPOISE

RAISIN D'ÊTRE

A CROSS DRESSER

SPOILED MILK

WORST ANEMONES

REFINED SUGARS

HAD I THE HEAVENS'
EMBROIDERED CLOTHS,
ENWROUGHT WITH
GOLDEN AND...

MIDDLE-AGED SPREAD

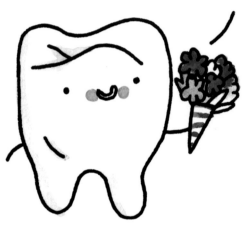

SWEET TOOTH

SOAP OPERA

CHILLY PEPPERS

SNAKE CHARMER

NOM DE PLUM

MATURE CHEDDAR

A TENNIS RACKET

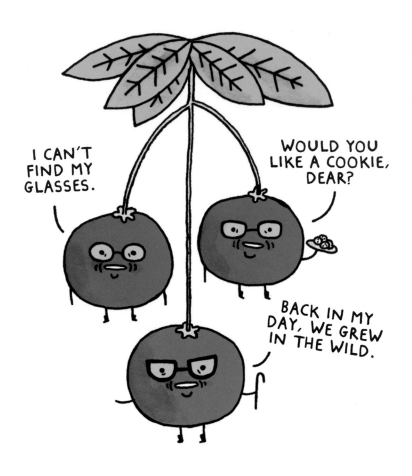

ELDERBERRIES

SENSITIVE TOOTHPASTE

MY LIFE IS
SO HARD!

mint

ORGAN RECITAL

SEASON'S GREETINGS

A BONE TO PICK

YAWN.

CAN'T BE BOTHERED.

LAZY BONES

I DIG THAT CRAZY BEAT, DADDY–O.

HIP BONES

WHY DID THE CHICKEN CROSS THE ROAD?

HUMERUS BONE

HUMBLE PIE

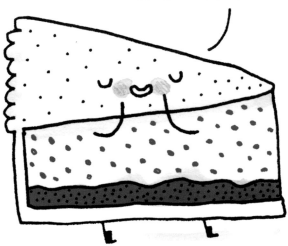

ME? DELICIOUS? AW, NO...
I'M JUST A LIL' OL' PIE TRYING
TO MAKE IT IN THIS CRUEL,
CRUEL WORLD.

STREAKY BACON

GUT FEELINGS

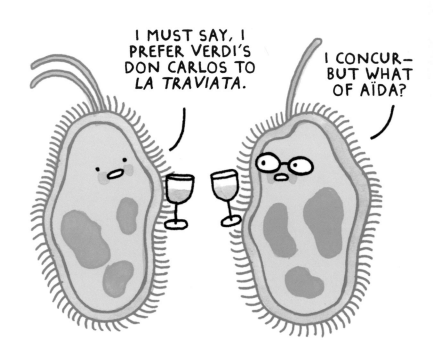

CULTURED BACTERIA

SOUR CREAM

ACKNOWLEDGMENTS

I'd like to thank my friends, family and pugs for putting up with my terrible sense of humour for all these years. In particular, thank you Anthony for providing pun-related critiques and also lunch. Thank you to everybody at Dog 'n' Bone and Cico Books, especially Pete Jorgensen, and to my friends at the Red Roaster, where the coffee is never bitter.

And thank you to whoever it was that made the cuddly toy Nessies that were for sale at Pitlochry Woolen Mill in Scotland during the 1990s. "Happi-Ness", "Grumpi-Ness" and their pals continue to inspire me as I embark on my punderful journey through life.